P9-APQ-257

Can the War on Terrorism Be Won?

Alison Jamieson

ARCTURUS

This edition first published by Arcturus Publishing
Distributed by Black Rabbit Books
P.O. Box 3263
Mankato
Minnesota MN 56002

Copyright © 2008 Arcturus Publishing Limited

Printed in the United States

All rights reserved.

Library of Congress Cataloging-in-Publication Data

Jamieson, Alison.
  Can the war on terrorism be won? /Alison Jamieson.
      p. cm. -- (Global questions)
ISBN 978-1-84837-014-2
1. Terrorism--Juvenile literature. 2. Terrorism--Prevention--Juvenile literature. I. Title.

HV6431.J327 2009
363.325--dc22

                           2008016661

9 8 7 6 5 4 3 2

The right of Alison Jamieson to be identified as the author of this work has been asserted by him/her in accordance with the Copyright, Designs and Patents Act 1988.

Series concept: Alex Woolf
Editor and picture researcher: Patience Coster
Designer: Ian Winton

Picture credits:
Corbis: 6 (Warrick Page), 7 (Sion Touhig), 8 (Bettmann), 10 (David Turnley), 14 (Leif Skoogfors), 18 (Bettmann), 19 (Reuters), 21 (Sean Adair/Reuters), 23 (Mohammed Jalil/epa), 25 (Reuters/Al Jazeera TV), 27 (Gideon Mendel), 28 (Peter MacDiarmid/Reuters), 29 (Reuters), 31 (Brooks Kraft), 33 (Syed Jan Sabawoon/epa), 34 (epa), 37 (Gideon Mendel), 38 (Tokyo Shimbun/Corbis Sygma), 40 (Richard Lewis/epa), 41 (Paul Faith/Pool/epa), 42 (Paul Hanna/Reuters). Mary Evans Picture Library: 9. Rex Features: 39 (Sipa Press). Shutterstock: 16, 26, 43. Topham Picturepoint: 13.

Cover: US Army guards escort a detainee at Camp X-ray in Cuba, a temporary holding facility for suspects captured after the terrorist attacks of 11 September 2001 and during the subsequent 'war on terrorism' (Brooks Kraft/Corbis).

Every attempt has been made to clear copyright. Should there be any inadvertent omission, please apply to the publisher for rectification.

Contents

Chapter 1

Should we have a war on terrorism?

What do you think of when you imagine a "war on terrorism"? Most likely the word *war* conjures up images of conflicts between countries, with soldiers in uniform fighting one another on land, at sea, and in the air. We tend to think of war as something that ends with the victory of one side over the other.

Army in the shadows

Terrorism is a difficult thing to have a war against. The terrorist enemy is hard to identify because terrorists work secretly, in silence, and wear no uniform. We may have an idea of where the leaders are, but the followers could be anywhere—in a far-off country or living in the street next to ours. Terrorists usually operate in small groups and lead seemingly normal lives. The terrorists' main weapon is surprise, and they can operate anywhere and at any time. Terrorists are engaged in a kind of war, but theirs is not what we would call a conventional war. Instead it is known as "asymmetric" warfare, or a battle between uneven forces. How, then, is it possible to wage a war on terrorism?

The word *terrorism* means the threat or use of violence to win certain rewards or goals. But we could say that bank robbers and bullies do this, so in what way are terrorists different? While bank robbery and

Pakistani soldiers stand guard on a mountain top, overlooking a valley recently occupied by Islamist militants. While the army has sophisticated equipment at its disposal, terrorists can easily hide in the rugged and vast landscape.

In London, United Kingdom (UK), police forensic officers gather evidence from a bus destroyed in the attacks of July 7, 2005. Four suicide bombers blew themselves up on the bus and three underground trains, killing 52 and injuring more than 700 people.

bullying involve private violence, or violence used for personal reasons, terrorism is different because it involves political violence. Terrorists have a set of aims, or political goals. They want to achieve these, not just for themselves, but for the country, community, or faith to which they belong. The political goals of terrorist groups vary, but they always concern the way in which a country or community is run, the person or people who are in charge, and the kind of laws that are obeyed. Terrorists are unhappy and angry about the way in which the community they claim to represent is treated. They believe that this unfair treatment prevents them from living freely and with dignity. Terrorists believe they have a just cause for their violent actions. They think their reasons for using violence are sound and the cause for which they are fighting is noble. They are also convinced that peaceful methods of protest do not work and that violence is the only way to change the situation.

FOCUS

Bomb attacks on London

On July 7, 2005, four men exploded bombs on the London transportation network. The men detonated backpack bombs on three underground trains and a bus, killing themselves and 52 other passengers. Shahzad Tanweer was one of the suicide bombers. Irshad Hussain was a friend of Shahzad's parents, Mumtaz and Parveen Tanweer. He simply could not understand how 22-year-old Shahzad had become involved in terrorism. Interviewed on the first anniversary of the bombings, Irshad said: "I knew Shahzad in the way that all Mumtaz's friends knew him: he was very intelligent, normal, polite—nothing to suggest he was a troublemaker. Shahzad's parents really, really looked after him. They gave him everything. He was doing well at university."

Making a point

Terrorists have a message they want to get across. This message is not necessarily directed at the people they threaten or use violence against. It is a warning to the organizations or governments who, in their opinion, are responsible for the unfair situation. The message says: "You may be more powerful than us, but we can use violence whenever we like, and we'll do so again if you don't do as we say." The message tells the people in charge to change their behavior—either to do something they have *not* been doing or to stop doing something they *have* been doing. In this sense, the politicians are the real target for the terrorists' message.

Sometimes terrorists kill an individual, such as a president or an important politician. He or she may be a symbol of what the terrorist group hates or is angry about. But terrorists can achieve the same or an even greater effect, with less effort, by killing or injuring ordinary people. This type of terrorist violence is indiscriminate, which means the terrorists do not care who the individuals are or what happens to them. These ordinary people who are victims of terrorism are often referred to as civilians, or non-combatants. They are unarmed and do not wear uniforms.

Former Italian premier Aldo Moro was kidnapped by the Red Brigades (Brigate Rosse), a left-wing terrorist group, on March 16, 1978. After holding Moro in captivity for 55 days, the group killed him.

Freedom struggles

Throughout history, there have been many instances where political freedom has been won through violence. In 1775, North America was a British colony, but many Americans felt they had little in common with the country that ruled them. They wanted to run things their own way. When Britain demanded that Americans pay a series of unpopular taxes, the people rebelled.

The head of King Louis XVI of France is shown to the Parisian crowd after his execution by guillotine in 1793. The word *terrorism* was first used during the "Reign of Terror" of the French Revolution.

In 1789, a violent revolution in France overthrew the monarchy and turned the country into a republic. Today this bloody period of French history is celebrated annually on July 14 with a public holiday, firework displays, and other festivities. The words *terrorism* and *terrorist* were first used during this time, but they had somewhat different meanings then. *La terreur*, or the "Reign of Terror," was a period in which France's new revolutionary leaders used terror as a method of holding on to power. In other words, terror was used *by* the leaders rather than *against* them. In the twentieth century, dictators such as Joseph Stalin in Russia and Adolf Hitler in Germany also used terrorism to strengthen their hold on power.

Expert View

For some people involved in a civil rights struggle against a brutal government, acts of terrorism seem justified:

"I was called a terrorist yesterday, but when I came out of jail, many people embraced me, including my enemies, and that is what I normally tell other people who say those who are struggling for liberation in their country are terrorists. I tell them that I was also a terrorist yesterday, but today, I am admired by the very people who said I was one."

Nelson Mandela, South African civil rights leader, speaking on May 16, 2000

Nelson Mandela voting in South Africa's first democratic elections in 1994. An anti-apartheid activist, Mandela was imprisoned for terrorist offenses in 1964. Twenty-seven years later, he was released. He went on to become South Africa's president and was hailed as a hero and peacemaker.

Different perceptions

Today most American people are proud of their history and most British people do not think of the country's revolutionary leader and first president, George Washington, as a terrorist. But perhaps it is easier to tolerate political violence that occurred long ago than to accept and explain violence that took place more recently or violence that is occurring today. In 1964, a South African court found civil rights activist Nelson Mandela guilty of being the leader of a terrorist group, the African National Congress (ANC). The court said that the aim of the group was to overthrow the South African apartheid government by force. Yet in 1993, Mandela was awarded the Nobel Peace Prize for his work in ending apartheid peacefully and bringing democracy to South Africa.

A just cause?

Most people believe that the African National Congress was fighting against oppression and for freedom in South Africa. The fight against apartheid, they would say, was a just cause. They might even say that "the end justifies the means." In other words: violence is acceptable if the cause is good. But this can be a dangerous attitude because it implies that it does not matter who is killed in the process—men, women, or children—if the cause is a good one. Furthermore, because people hold very different political views, they will never agree on what is a "just cause." Some people will argue that those committing the violence are right to do so; other people will argue the complete opposite. We need to disregard these political arguments. A balanced view of what constitutes a "terrorist act" can only be reached by focusing on *what* terrorists *do* (their methods) and to *whom* they do it.

If terrorism is violence or the threat of violence against civilians, should we and can we wage war on it? Surely declaring a war on terrorism is like declaring war on a *method* of conflict. Conflicts between states have always existed, and there have always been groups or communities within states who feel they are badly treated and who will fight against their rulers. Of course, it is vital to do everything we can to prevent and combat terrorism. But it may never go away completely, and those fighting it can never be sure of victory or defeat.

FORUM

The notion of what terrorism is and who terrorists are differs according to people's beliefs, culture, and the degree of power they hold:

"The difference between the revolutionary and the terrorist lies in the reasons for which each fights. For whoever stands by a just cause and fights for the freedom and liberation of his land from the invaders, the settlers and the colonialists cannot possibly be called terrorist."

Palestinian leader Yasser Arafat, addressing the UN General Assembly, November 13, 1974. Arafat spent most of his life in armed struggle against Israel in an attempt to establish an independent Palestinian homeland. He was described by many as a terrorist but later renounced violence and campaigned for peace in the Middle East.

"I cannot agree that a terrorist can ever be an idealist, or that the objects sought can ever justify terrorism. The impact of terrorism . . . is intrinsically [utterly] evil, necessarily evil, and wholly evil."

Benjamin Netanyahu, former Israeli prime minister

Do you think people who use violence to bring about political change are terrorists?

Chapter 2

Who are the "terrorists" of history?

The first "terrorists" lived in the first century CE and belonged to a Jewish sect called Zealots. They lived in an area of the Middle East (now Israel), which was then part of the Roman Empire. The Zealots fiercely resisted Roman occupation and killed other Jews who collaborated with the occupiers.

Assassins and thugs

The Assassins lived in eleventh-century Syria and Persia (now Iran). A Muslim sect, they fought against rulers who threatened their way of life and freedom of worship. The word *assassin*, Arabic for "hashish eater," came into our language at this time. The Assassins were believed to inhale pipes full of hashish before departing on their "sacred mission" of murder. Using daggers as weapons, they tried to kill their enemies in crowded public places on public holidays, with many people watching.

The Thugs of India were a murderous Hindu sect, active for 600 years until about 1830. They usually chose travelers as their victims, killing them as sacrifices to the Hindu goddess Kali. A Thug would appear to befriend his victim during a long journey, then strangle him with a silk tie. The word *thug* comes from the Hindi *thag*, meaning "rogue" or "deceiver." Like *assassin*, *thug* remains part of our vocabulary of violence.

Expert View

Two historians offer very different opinions about the suffragette revolt:

"Suffragette terrorism did not only fail to win the vote: it alienated public opinion, threw away the moral advantage, and became a positive obstruction to votes for women because no government could appear to surrender to political violence."

C. J. Bearman, BBC History *magazine, February 2007*

"The suffragettes were not terrorists but radical fighters in a just cause."

June Purvis, BBC History *magazine, February 2007*

By the summer of 1914, over 1,000 suffragettes had been imprisoned in the UK for crimes committed in the cause of women's rights. Women were not granted voting rights until 1918.

Anarchists and suffragettes

The early terrorists used violence for religious reasons. But the first group of "modern" terrorists, who lived in Russia in the nineteenth century, used violence for political reasons. Known as anarchists, they wanted to overthrow the Russian rulers, or tsars, in a revolution and were early examples of "left-wing" terrorists (see chapter 3).

In Britain at the start of the twentieth century, a group of women known as suffragettes began a series of non-violent protests to draw attention to their lack of suffrage (voting rights). Suffragettes disrupted election rallies and chained themselves to the railings of Buckingham Palace and 10 Downing Street in London, the home of the prime minister. Most leading politicians of the day were opposed to giving women the vote, believing that "their natural sphere is not the turmoil and dust of politics, but the circle of social and domestic life."

In 1909, suffragettes began to use violence to attract more press and public interest to their cause. They broke the windows of government buildings and set fire to cricket pavilions, golf clubhouses, and racecourse stands. They poured acid and ink into mailboxes and set fire to letters. They slashed paintings and damaged statues in art galleries. They threatened members of Parliament and damaged their homes. Their leader, Emmeline Pankhurst, said that "all the methods of war" could be used in the battle for the vote, although human (and animal) life was to be held sacred. The press talked of "madwomen," and "dangerous and wicked violence" carried out by "terrorists." Many who had supported the suffragettes did not agree with their campaigns of violence, and the movement divided.

When World War I broke out in 1914, most of the suffragettes decided to support their country. Thousands of women went to work in factories and shipyards and on buses, taking on jobs that had traditionally been done by men. In February 1918, the British government passed a law giving women over the age of 30 the right to vote. Women over the age of 21 were eventually given equal voting rights with men in 1928.

Terrorism in Northern Ireland

The Irish Republican Army (IRA) was founded during Ireland's struggle for independence from Britain between 1919 and 1922. Its successor, the Provisional IRA, was formed in 1969. Its aim was to defend the minority Catholic population in Northern Ireland, to drive out the British by force, and eventually to reunite Northern Ireland with republican southern Ireland.

In the 1960s, Protestants in Northern Ireland had access to better houses, schools, and jobs than Catholics. The Catholic Civil Rights Association demanded equal rights and held protest marches. In January 1972, the British army opened fire on a peaceful demonstration in Londonderry, a town

In 1972, a paint factory burns after being bombed by the IRA in Belfast, Northern Ireland. The IRA wanted a Northern Ireland free from British interests and influence and attacked people or property that were symbols of British rule.

in Northern Ireland. Thirteen Catholics were killed. A few months later, the IRA exploded 22 bombs in Belfast, killing nine people. The IRA bombing campaign continued for 30 years. Its principal targets were British soldiers and other symbols of British rule, but many civilians were killed and injured too. Loyalist Protestant terror groups were also formed. Their aim was to keep Northern Ireland as part of the UK and to fight the nationalist groups who wanted reunification. More than 3,000 people were killed between 1969 and the mid-1990s, about two-thirds of them by the IRA and one-third by the loyalist terror groups.

The ANC

In South Africa, the African National Congress was founded as a political party to defend the rights of black South Africans, who were discriminated against under the system of apartheid. When black people tried to protest peacefully, they were often arrested, beaten, or killed. In 1960, 69 black people were killed during a peaceful protest. ANC leaders, including Nelson Mandela, decided that "armed struggle" was necessary for things to change. They began with the sabotage of government property and machinery. Mandela was arrested in 1962 and in 1964 was sent to prison for life. During Mandela's imprisonment, the conflict became more violent on both sides.

The government imprisoned thousands of people without trial and tortured many of them. The ANC detonated bombs in public buildings and cars, killing civilians.

After many years, white South Africans began to realize that apartheid could not last. The United Nations (UN), world governments, and public opinion agreed that it was a cruel and unjust regime. Nelson Mandela was released from prison, and the apartheid laws were gradually abolished. South Africa held its first democratic elections in 1994. The ANC won the most votes and formed a government, and Nelson Mandela was elected as the country's president.

FORUM

The quotes below illustrate the view that "one person's terrorist is another person's freedom fighter":

"The ANC is a typical terrorist organization … Anyone who thinks it is going to run the government in South Africa is living in cloud cuckoo land."

British prime minister Margaret Thatcher, 1987

"Nelson Mandela is the most inspired, the greatest and most courageous leader of our generation. This is the man who will be remembered forever as the leader who ended apartheid … the leader who became a liberator, who always chose reconciliation above revenge, who symbolized the fight against racial tyranny and the protection of human rights."

British Prime Minister Gordon Brown, 2007

Why do you think these two British prime ministers have such different views?

Chapter 3

What do terrorists want?

Terrorists want to bring about political change. Usually this means they want to replace one kind of government or set of laws with another. Over the centuries, religious groups have used terrorism to draw attention to their cause. Although these groups appear to act out of religious belief, their grievances are often political as well as religious.

Left-wing terrorism

In the 1960s, 1970s, and 1980s, at the height of the Cold War, left-wing terrorism was common in parts of Latin America and Western Europe. This type of terrorism was inspired by a set of beliefs called communism. The two most important political thinkers behind communism were German writer Karl Marx (1818–83) and Chinese leader Mao Zedong (1893–1976). According to communist doctrine, the working classes (in industrial countries) and the peasants (in rural societies) should seize power by force and take over their country. The aim of this communist revolution was to give everyone

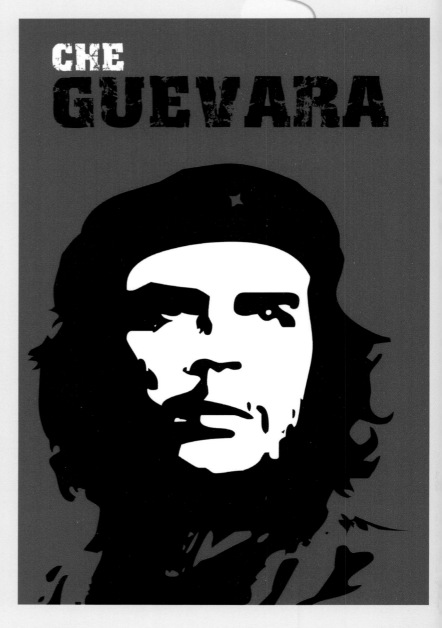

Guerrilla fighter Che Guevara became an icon for a generation of left-wing thinkers, including terrorist groups. His image appeared on posters and T-shirts.

a share in the country's wealth and the chance to decide how the country was run.

Argentine-born Ernesto "Che" Guevara was a famous Latin American guerrilla leader who helped to bring about a revolution in Cuba in 1959 that swept communist leader Fidel Castro to power. Che was a hero to Western European left-wing terrorist groups such as the German Red Army Faction and the Italian Red Brigades. Che's early death in 1967 at the hands of his enemies in Bolivia made him a martyr in the eyes of these groups. In the 1970s, the groups tried, and failed, to organize the working classes in their countries to bring about a revolution. European left-wing terrorists kidnapped, killed, and injured politicians, judges, and businessmen who they perceived to be symbols of power and corruption, but generally they avoided indiscriminate attacks against civilians.

FOCUS

Thoughts of a former terrorist

Adriana Faranda belonged to the Italian left-wing terrorist group the Red Brigades. She was involved in several terrorist attacks in Rome. In 1979, she was arrested and spent many years in prison. In a prison interview, she tried to explain how terrorists are able to go out and kill people in cold blood. She said they held their victims responsible for everything they hated about Italian society: "the real unhappiness of people, deaths at the workplace, homeless earthquake victims, kids who die of heroin because someone allows it to happen, and also our own friends, comrades killed by the police during demonstrations." But her years in prison changed Adriana, and she came to believe "that violence can actually make you unclean too, that violence only leads to violence—it's not true that violence can purify anything; every time you use violence, you diminish yourself. "

Right-wing terrorism

Right-wing terrorism occurred mostly in the 1970s and 1980s. Right-wing terrorists are often admirers of "strong-arm" leaders such as Adolf Hitler. They do not believe in equal rights or democratic government. Their aim is to frighten people into demanding a strict government of law and order. Right-wing attacks have usually been indiscriminate bomb attacks in crowded public places or on trains. For example, in August 1980 in the Bologna, Italy, train station, a bomb exploded, killing 85 people, and in September 1980 a bomb attack at the Munich beer festival in Germany killed 13. The two attacks were not linked.

State and state-sponsored terrorism

Sometimes a country's rulers have employed a "reign of terror" to strengthen their control. Dictators who have used state terrorism in this way include Adolf Hitler in Germany, Joseph Stalin in the Soviet Union, and Saddam Hussein in Iraq. At times, governments also secretly help terrorist groups by giving them money, weapons, or training. This is known as state-sponsored terrorism and occurs when the government and terrorist group share the same goal. For example, they might want the same political leader assassinated or the same government overthrown. During the Cold War, the US Central Intelligence Agency (CIA) helped right-wing terrorist groups in countries with left-wing governments such as Cuba, Chile, Nicaragua, and Vietnam. In turn, agents of communist governments gave support to left-wing terrorists in Germany and the Middle East.

The Nazis skillfully used huge rallies of uniformed followers to intimidate their opponents. Hitler also used state terrorism against his own people when he authorized the extermination of millions of German Jews.

Ideas of freedom

All terrorists say they want "freedom" for the society they represent. Ayman Al Zawahiri, deputy leader of the terrorist organization Al Qaeda, has called for "the freedom of the Muslim lands and their liberation from every aggressor." For some groups in the United States, freedom is the right of every adult to buy, sell, and carry guns without restriction. In the mid-1990s, some of these groups, or militias, believed that the United Nations was plotting to form a world government and that it would prevent ordinary Americans from keeping guns. Timothy McVeigh, a militia member, was convinced that the federal authorities wanted to ban all privately owned firearms. He decided to give them a warning not to do so. In early 1995, he visited various federal government buildings in different US cities to see where a bomb would have maximum impact. On April 19, he parked a truck full of explosives outside the Alfred P. Murrah Federal Building in Oklahoma City. He exploded the truck by remote control. The bombing killed 168 people.

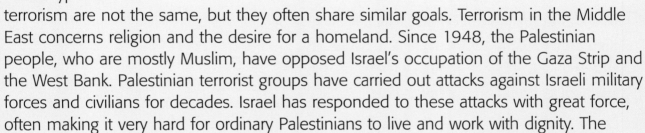

The Alfred P. Murrah Federal Building in Oklahoma City following the truck bomb attack of April 19, 1995. Of the 168 victims, 19 were children, most of whom perished when the bomb blast destroyed the building's day-care centre.

Nationalist and religious terrorism

These types of terrorism are not the same, but they often share similar goals. Terrorism in the Middle East concerns religion and the desire for a homeland. Since 1948, the Palestinian people, who are mostly Muslim, have opposed Israel's occupation of the Gaza Strip and the West Bank. Palestinian terrorist groups have carried out attacks against Israeli military forces and civilians for decades. Israel has responded to these attacks with great force, often making it very hard for ordinary Palestinians to live and work with dignity. The failure to solve the Arab-Israeli conflict in the Middle East has led to tension between Western and Muslim countries. Some Muslims think the West wants to destroy Islam. They believe they need to defend themselves by attacking Western interests. This is the belief of the Al Qaeda organization, which many people consider to be today's greatest terrorist threat.

Expert View

Ayatollah Khomeini was the spiritual and political leader of a revolution that saw the overthrow of the shah of Iran in 1979. Like many revolutionaries, the ayatollah believed he had the right to speak for his nation as a whole:

"What the nation wants is an Islamic republic. Not just a republic, not a democratic republic, not a democratic Islamic republic. Just an Islamic republic. Do not use the word *democratic*. That is Western, and we do not want it."

Ayatollah Khomeini, leader of the Iranian revolution, 1979

Al Qaeda

The name *Al Qaeda* means "the base." Al Qaeda wants to be the base or starting point for an Islamic revolution that will result in Muslim countries being governed solely by Islamic law. Al Qaeda has two main goals: the first is to rid all Muslim countries of foreigners and foreign influences; the second is to create a huge Islamic state in which Muslims are part of one community, or *umma*. This state is to be ruled by Islamic sharia law. Al Qaeda members believe that democracy is a bad form of government because it is "man-made" and does not come directly from God. Many Muslims around the world believe that religion and law should be one and the same and that it is wrong to separate the two. However, in Europe and the United States, religion and law are separate, and Muslims living in these parts of the world accept this fact. Of course, most Muslims do not support Al Qaeda but want to live in peace with other religions.

Al Qaeda has stated that its main enemy is the United States and any countries that support the United States militarily. There are several reasons for this. First, the United States has sent soldiers to occupy Muslim countries, including Afghanistan and Iraq, where Muslims have been killed and injured. Al Qaeda says that this is terrorism. Second, the United States supports Israel, and Israel occupies land that Muslims say should belong to the Palestinians. Israeli forces have killed many Muslims in the Palestinian territories (but many Israeli soldiers and civilians have also been killed by Palestinian bombers and suicide bombers). Third, according to Al Qaeda,

FORUM

For the jihadists, the attacks of September 11, 2001, that destroyed the World Trade Center and killed around 3,000 people were acts of bravery. But the US government and the victims' relatives saw them as brutal acts of cowardice:

"On the blessed Tuesday September 11, 2001 … they launched their attacks with their planes in an unparalleled and magnificent feat of valor, unmatched by any humankind before them."

Osama bin Laden, posted on an Islamist website, February 14, 2003

"We will make no distinction between the terrorists who committed these acts and those who harbor them … Make no mistake, the United States will hunt down and punish those responsible for these cowardly acts."

George W. Bush, after the events of September 11, 2001

Heroes or cowards—what do you think?

An attack aimed at the United States' financial heart: on September 11, 2001, hijacked United Airlines flight 175 flies toward the South Tower of the World Trade Center in New York City. The North Tower burns from the impact of the first hijacked plane that crashed into it 15 minutes earlier.

Western society wants to corrupt Muslims, make them dishonest and wicked, and encourage them to lose respect for Islamic laws. Al Qaeda believes that a war is going on, with Muslims on one side and Christians and Jews on the other. It believes Muslims have a duty to attack American people—soldiers and civilians—and anyone else who supports the United States. Its attacks are part of a jihad, or holy war, to save Islam and keep it pure. So this type of terrorism cannot be called "Islamic" terrorism because most Muslims do not support it; instead it is known as jihadi terrorism.

Chapter 4

How has terrorism changed?

In recent years, there have been four major changes in what terrorists do and how they do it. They are the result of advances in communications technology and a change in the strategies (political direction) and tactics (methods) of jihadi terrorist groups.

A different structure

In the past, most terrorist groups had a pyramid structure. At the top of this structure was a leadership group responsible for the organization's strategy and tactics. At the next level were individuals responsible for specific tasks, including fund-raising; acquiring weapons; "logistics" such as food, accommodations, and travel; and recruitment and training. Below this were the local leaders. At the base of the pyramid were the ordinary operatives, or foot soldiers. The organization might have had cells in different places, but it was coordinated and managed from a central location.

Terrorism analysts believe that this structure is rare today: first, because it is too risky to base the important functions of an illegal organization in one place and second, because there is no need to do so since technology allows terrorists to communicate safely and quickly and move around the world with ease. The pyramid structure has been replaced by loosely linked, largely independent networks. There may still be a main source of authority or finance and fixed sites such as training camps, but experts believe that most terrorists now work in small, locally based cells. They have jobs, lead apparently ordinary lives, and do not arouse suspicion. They decide their strategy, tactics, targets, and time frame for action and possibly even organize their own fund-raising.

Expert View

Analysts believe that the structure of terrorist organizations has altered from pyramid to network, making groups difficult to trace and track:

"Each node in a network may refer to an individual, a group, an institution, part of a group or institution, or even a state ... The organizational design is flat. Ideally there is no single, central leadership, command, or headquarters—no precise heart or head that can be targeted."

J. Arquilla and D. Ronfeldt, **The Advent of Netwar: Analytic Background**

Mass casualties

It used to be thought that terrorists' main aim was to gain support and publicity for their cause; they did not want to make themselves unpopular by killing a lot of people. However, statements made by jihadi groups in recent years have made it clear that they want to kill as many "infidels" as possible. Mass casualty attacks can certainly be used to great effect. The killing of 3,000 people stirs up much more fear than the killing of three. If terrorists also carry out multiple mass casualty attacks, as they did by hijacking four separate aircraft on September 11, 2001, or by bombing three underground trains and a bus in one hour in London in July 2005, the impact is even stronger.

Suicide attacks

Terrorist suicide attacks, or "martyrdom operations," are not new. During World War II, Japanese kamikaze pilots flew their aircraft into enemy ships, and in the 1980s, there were suicide attacks in Lebanon and Sri Lanka. However, the frequency with which such operations now occur has increased. Almost three-quarters of all recorded suicide attacks have taken place since the 9/11 attacks on Washington, DC, and New York. There have been nearly 1,000 suicide attacks in Iraq since the United States led an invasion of that country in 2003, and they are becoming increasingly frequent in Afghanistan.

The shoe of a female suicide bomber lies at the scene of an attack in the Karrada district of central Baghdad, Iraq. Suicide bombings are hard to prevent and are an effective and terrifying form of terrorist attack.

Suicide operations, like mass casualty attacks, are designed to shock. People feel terrified and helpless in the face of what appears to be fanatical criminal behavior that cannot even be punished because the terrorist always takes his or her own life, along with many others. The operations are cheap and effective, especially for a small organization fighting a powerful government or army. It costs about $150 to stage an average Palestinian suicide bomb attack. The London bombings—including overseas travel, bomb-making equipment, and car rental for the attackers—probably cost less than $12,500. Jihadi leaders frequently stress the "nobility" of death and martyrdom and train militants to prepare for these missions. Volunteers are not depressed or "suicidal" but proud and confident that they will receive their reward in paradise. They believe they are doing God's will.

Expert View

Analysts say that terrorist organizations look on suicide attacks as an extremely effective way of showing their ability and determination to use violence:

"Suicide tactics have been adopted by a growing number of terrorist organizations around the world because they are shocking, deadly, cost effective, secure, and very difficult to stop. There are only two basic operational requirements that an organization must be able to satisfy to get into the game: a willingness to kill and a willingness to die."

Bruce Hoffman, **Inside Terrorism**

Technological advances

Terrorists take full advantage of the high-tech tools now available. Technology helps them to protect themselves and their activities, to spread their message, and to recruit new members. According to US intelligence, Al Qaeda has state-of-the-art equipment for communicating, tracking, intercepting, and hacking and also has the skills to use it.

Cyberspace has been called the "new Wild West." Terrorists can encrypt messages and transfer money electronically. They can discuss plans and tactics using e-mail and Internet chat rooms protected by firewalls. Because the Internet is largely unregulated, each terrorist group can have its own website. Jihadi websites show the destruction of lives and property by Western troops in Afghanistan and Iraq. They explain what jihad is and show video footage of soldiers and civilians being killed in Iraq. This is meant to encourage young men to leave their homes and fight. The sites are in several languages as well as Arabic and are mostly aimed at young, middle-class Muslims in the West.

Al-Jazeera
Exclusive

خاص
بالجزيرة

أولى
حروب القرن

أسامة بن لادن
زعيم تنظيم القاعدة

Al Qaeda leader Osama bin Laden appears in a taped message broadcast on the Arabic television station Al Jazeera in 2001. Bin Laden is considered to be the world's most wanted fugitive.

The Internet has also changed the way terrorists are recruited. Recruitment used to take place in mosques or religious training schools, but now many young people go through a process of "self-recruitment" via the Internet. Combat training manuals, firearms training, and bomb-making instructions are all available to download, leading to a kind of do-it-yourself terrorism. Palestinian terrorists admitted using the Google Earth website to map targets for rocket strikes on Israel. British officials say Al Qaeda used the same site to find targets inside British bases near the city of Basra in southern Iraq. In March 2004, jihadi terrorists used cell phones to detonate bombs on four trains in Madrid, Spain, killing 191 people. When police raided an apartment used by the group, they found on a computer hard drive instructions downloaded from the Internet on how to detonate bombs using cell phones.

FORUM

Experts used to say that terrorists wanted publicity above anything. But modern terrorists seem to be saying something different:

"Terrorists want a lot of people watching, not a lot of people dead."

Brian M. Jenkins, terrorism expert, 1975

"We do not have tanks or rockets, but we have something superior—our exploding Islamic human bombs. In place of a nuclear arsenal, we are proud of our arsenal of believers."

A member of Hamas's al-Qassam Brigades in Gaza

Do you think terrorism has changed?

Chapter 5

How can we fight terrorism?

Most people agree that the "tool kit" of measures to fight terrorism should include many different elements. The UK's counter-terrorism strategy is built on four "pillars" or rules.

Closed-circuit TV surveillance at harbours, airports and train stations is one means of monitoring suspicious activities, but are we being 'spied on' too much?

The first pillar says that people must be prevented from being drawn into terrorism. The second says that people who become involved in planning, supporting, and carrying out attacks must be pursued. The third says that communications, transportation networks, and essential services must be protected. And the fourth says that preparation must be made for managing the consequences of attacks.

Using the law

The law is a vital weapon in the fight against terrorism. It is used to help prevent terrorism, to investigate attacks, and punish those responsible. Since 2000, the UK government has brought in four separate laws on terrorism. The Terrorism Act 2006 made it a crime to commit acts in preparation for terrorism, to encourage others to commit acts of terrorism, or to "glorify" terrorism. It also made it illegal to print, sell, or distribute terrorist publications and to give or receive terrorist training.

The police and intelligence services work constantly to prevent and detect acts of terrorism. They use "target hardening," which involves the protection of people and places that terrorists might attack. Airports, aircraft, train stations, public buildings,

Armed police, like this officer at Victoria Station in London, are now a regular sight in Britain, where the terror alert remains at a critical level.

monuments, and certain public figures are closely guarded to make acts of terrorism harder to commit. The law allows police and intelligence services to use special methods to detect serious crime. They can employ surveillance to see where a suspect goes and whom he or she meets. They can put a wiretap on a suspect's telephone or an electronic eavesdropping device inside a house, office, or car to listen in on conversations. They can, with special permission, monitor private e-mail and Internet traffic.

Another way they obtain information is by infiltrating suspected terrorist groups. This means that a police officer or intelligence officer will pretend to join the group and share its goals. He or she will listen to the planning for terrorist activity, and then prevent it from happening. The person who infiltrates will have to make dangerous and difficult decisions, not least of which will be whether to intervene immediately or whether to wait until the point at which as many terrorists as possible can be caught.

The Patriot Act

The US government responded to the terrorist attacks of 9/11 with a law called the Patriot Act. This gave more powers to law enforcement agencies to track and intercept communications and search private records. It made it easier to gather information about terrorist suspects and detain or deport immigrants on suspicion of terrorism. In the United States, the homes and businesses of a suspect can be searched without the permission or knowledge of their owner. Some people feel this law is too severe because it restricts civil liberties; others feel it is justified in the fight against terrorism.

Expert View

As analysts observe, people have high expectations of those who are fighting terrorism:

"Fighting terrorism is like being a goalkeeper. You can make a hundred brilliant saves, but the only shot that people remember is the one that gets past you."

Paul Wilkinson, Daily Telegraph, September 1, 1992

International agreement

Ideally, laws against terrorism should be agreed to at the international level. If one country regards hijacking an aircraft or giving money to a terrorist organization as a crime but another country does not, then it can be more difficult to prevent such terrorist acts. The United Nations has therefore drawn up 13 anti-terrorism conventions (international laws). Each country that signs the conventions promises to make efforts to prevent, detect, and punish certain crimes.

The countries of the European Union (EU) have agreed on measures to prevent and detect terrorism. Within Europe, arrested terrorist suspects can be transferred quickly to the country that wants to investigate them. Since 2006, telephone companies and Internet service providers have been required to store records of customer communications for up to two years. In November 2007, the European Commission made new proposals. If these are agreed to, all 27 EU members will make the recruitment, training, and encouragement of terrorists illegal. It would become a crime to set up websites that encourage violence or explain how to make bombs.

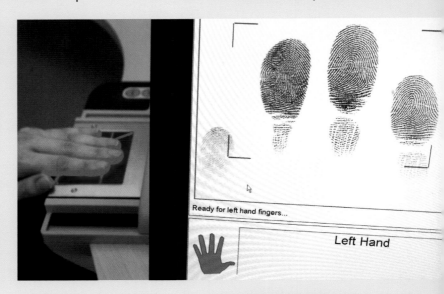

Ready for left hand fingers...

Left Hand

A British Passport Office volunteer has his fingerprints scanned for an identity card. In 2004, the British government announced plans to introduce identity cards, but many people oppose them, believing they will not stop terrorist attacks.

Using the military

Military action is another instrument in the anti-terrorism tool kit. In October 2001, US and UK forces bombed Afghanistan when Taliban leaders refused to hand over Osama bin Laden, considered to be the mastermind of the 9/11 attacks in the United States. Sometimes military force can be necessary, but great caution is required. Military action tends to be heavy-handed and does not always take sufficient account of the civilian population, who may have nothing to do with terrorism. If the search for terrorists results in civilian deaths or destruction of property, the population will not support the anti-terrorist actions and may well be hostile to them.

Women working for peace

Women often suffer the most in periods of conflict. During the 1994 genocide in Rwanda, many of the victims were women and children. In war-torn countries, women's experience is recognized as essential in rebuilding peace. In Rwanda's first election under a new constitution in 2003, women accounted for 49 percent of those elected, the highest of any parliament in the world. Mary Balikungeri is the founder of the Rwanda Women's Network. This organization helps women who have suffered from war and looks for peaceful solutions to conflict.

Ms. Balinkungeri and 15 other women from all over Africa were invited to tour the United States to talk about their work. Some of the women were from countries that were at war with one another. Mary Balikungeri said: "You come to realize that we need each other. All of us, regardless of where we were from, saw that everywhere women are the victims."

Involving citizens

Terrorism arises from people's grievances—their problems and their sense of being unjustly treated. In a democracy, citizens can participate in political decision making through local councils, organizations, and political movements. Television and newspapers give space to local or national protests. Governments can listen to grievances and make changes to avoid the protests turning into terrorism (though problems are harder to resolve successfully in undemocratic countries).

In October 2001, two boys stand on the ruins of a house destroyed by a stray US bomb in a town north of the Afghan capital, Kabul. Using military force against terrorism is risky because civilians may be killed or injured in the process.

Tackling injustice

Governments need to be aware of inequalities. If some members of society have much better jobs, schools, houses, and pay than others, it is more likely that people will feel resentful and angry and will start to express their anger in violent behavior. This is even more likely in societies where a large proportion of the population is under the age of 30, because young people are usually quicker to show their anger. Governments need to encourage social policies and programs that make everyone feel he or she belongs to and has a stake in the same society. This means creating a sense of shared citizenship that crosses the barriers of race, language, and religion.

Police and intelligence services alone cannot prevent terrorism: the public must be involved. People selling chemicals or substances that could be used to make explosives are asked to report any large or suspicious transactions. This is because terrorists have acquired everyday products such as nail polish, fertilizer, and hair bleach for use in explosive devices. Citizens are also asked to keep their eyes open when they travel, to report suspicious packages if they see them, and to inform the police of any unusual activities in their neighborhood. If local communities are to work together with the police, there must be respect and trust on both sides.

FORUM

Across the world, attitudes differ about how to fight terrorism effectively:

"Terrorism wins only if you respond to it in the way that the terrorists want you to … If you choose not to respond at all or else to respond in a way different from that which they desire, they will fail to achieve their objectives."

David Fromkin, The Strategy of Terrorism

"We do not create terrorism by fighting the terrorists. We invite terrorism by ignoring them."

President George W. Bush, December 18, 2005

What's your view?

Dangers

Not everyone agrees about how strict the laws on terrorism should be. Most people feel there should be a balance. They do not want to be "spied on" by closed-circuit TV or have their emails read by others. But these are tools that might prevent terrorism. The question is, how far are we prepared to accept limitations on our freedom in order to make society safer from terrorists? If laws become too strict, with, for example, armed police on our street corners and tanks outside our airports, it shows that we are afraid. Then the terrorists will have achieved their aims,

A prisoner being marched out at the US-run detention center Camp X-Ray, at Guantánamo Bay in Cuba. Hundreds of terror suspects have been held here as enemy combatants but they have not been charged or put on trial. Many people think this treatment is unlawful.

and terrorism will have "worked." If it is legal to arrest a peaceful demonstrator and accuse him or her of terrorism, then civil liberties are in danger of being eroded. If Congress or a parliament passes laws that keep people in prison without being charged or going to trial for years, then democracy is in danger of being undermined. If torture is used to defend democracy, then the torturers become as bad as the terrorists. Terrorists *want* governments to overreact. If democracies break their own rules, then the terrorists can say their actions are a form of self-defense. It is important for societies and governments to hold on to the things they value, such as respect for human rights and the right to a fair trial.

Chapter 6

Are we winning the fight against terrorism?

The so-called global war on terror began with the US-led invasion of Afghanistan in October 2001. Since then, there have been successes as well as failures. While those involved cannot yet claim to be winning, there is some evidence to suggest that progress is being made.

The invasion of Afghanistan

After the 9/11 attacks, Taliban leaders in Afghanistan refused to give up Al Qaeda leader Osama bin Laden, whom they were protecting. By invading Afghanistan, the US-led coalition aimed to capture Bin Laden, destroy Al Qaeda, and remove the Taliban from power. By December 2001, the Taliban had been defeated, and since then, the International Security Assistance Force (ISAF) has been based in Afghanistan. Its aim is to help the country to become a stable, peaceful democracy. However, although democratic elections have been held and the country has a new constitution, it cannot yet be called stable or peaceful. Al Qaeda has not been defeated, and jihadi terrorism has increased. Between 2001 and 2003, terror attacks caused hundreds of deaths in Tunisia, Saudi Arabia, Pakistan, Indonesia, Turkey, and Morocco. These attacks were mostly aimed at Western people who were working or on vacation in these mainly Muslim countries.

In 2002, the Taliban began to return to Afghanistan, especially to the southern and eastern provinces. Since 2003, there has been fierce fighting here between Taliban and ISAF forces (the latter working with units of the Afghan army). In 2007, attacks increased by 60 percent in Helmand Province, where Taliban support is strongest.

Expert View

US government representatives appear certain of the nature of the terrorist threat:

"We are facing a persistent terrorist enemy led by Al Qaeda that remains driven and intent on attacking the homeland and that continues to adapt and improve its capabilities."

Spokeswoman for the White House, July 17, 2007

Pakistani tribal elders arrive at Kabul International Airport to attend a joint Pakistan-Afghanistan assembly. Pakistan shares a border with Afghanistan. Dialogue between the two countries is vital in order to bring peace to the region.

Toward the end of 2007, President Hamid Karzai began looking for new ways to bring peace to Afghanistan. His aim is to build up trust between local tribal leaders, the Afghan authorities, and the international forces supporting them. The idea is to win the "hearts and minds" of the local population so that they no longer support the extremist groups among the Taliban or give help to Al Qaeda. This strategy does not involve talks between Al Qaeda and the Afghan government; instead, it involves talks between groups who have contacts and influence with both sides and who may include former Taliban fighters. These groups can influence local populations to support democracy rather than insurgency and terrorism.

The invasion of Iraq

In March 2003, US and UK forces invaded Iraq and overthrew the regime of the Iraqi president, Saddam Hussein. In addition, Australia, Poland, Spain, the Netherlands, Denmark, and Italy sent large numbers of troops to occupy Iraq after the invasion. Some people said that Saddam Hussein might have been involved in the 9/11 attacks, that he had weapons of mass destruction (WMD), and that he might sell them to terrorists. The Al Qaeda leadership was not allied to Saddam Hussein, but it decided to support Iraq, a Muslim land. During the invasion, US bombs and missiles destroyed Iraqi towns and villages and many lives were lost. In December 2004, Bin Laden described the Iraq conflict as a "golden and unique opportunity" for jihadists to attack and defeat the United States.

Mourners pray beside the coffins of the victims of a suicide bomb attack at a mosque in Fallujah, Iraq. Religious tensions in Iraq remain a major problem.

Terrorists in Iraq

Al Qaeda and its supporters in other Muslim countries started to use Iraq as a base for attacks against Western military forces and civilians. Al Qaeda in Iraq has also encouraged fighting between the country's two main religious groups, Sunnis and Shias. Like Afghanistan, Iraq has held elections and has a new constitution, but the tensions between the Sunnis and Shias have increased. Iraq is a very divided country, the level of violence remains high, and its political leaders cannot govern effectively. Of the 4.5 million Iraqis who fled the country, only about 20,000 have returned, but some feel the tide may be turning.

Expert View

The head of the US forces in Iraq is optimistic that the situation is improving there:

"The most significant development in the past six months has been the increasing emergence of tribes and local citizens rejecting Al Qaeda and other extremists. We engaged in dialogue with insurgent groups and tribes. And this led to additional elements standing up to oppose Al Qaeda and other extremists."

General David Petraeus, US commander in Iraq, December 2007

Al Qaeda seems to be losing support, especially in the province of al-Anbar, where violence decreased in the second half of 2007. In October 2007, the US ambassador to Iraq said that Al Qaeda had "simply gone" from some areas. In the Iraqi capital, Baghdad, stores, offices, and restaurants have reopened. There is less violence, weddings are celebrated, and children play in the streets again.

Western Europe and the United States

Many people believe that the war in Iraq has been a cause of more terrorism around the world, especially against countries that supported the invasion. Spain sent 1,300 troops to Iraq in August 2003. On March 11, 2004, four commuter trains were bombed in the Spanish capital, Madrid, killing 191 people and wounding 2,000. In July 2005, four suicide bombers detonated bombs on three underground trains and a bus during the London rush hour (see page 7). This marked a terrible "first" in terrorism: it was the first suicide attack in Europe, and all four bombers were British citizens.

FOCUS

Counting the cost

Life for ordinary Iraqis is full of danger and difficulties. The organization Oxfam International reports that 70 percent of Iraqis lack access to safe drinking water and 43 percent live on less than one dollar a day. Many doctors have fled the country, and hospitals cannot cope with all the sick and injured people who come for help. Internet blogs provide a way for some young Iraqis to communicate with one another and the outside world and to share their problems. One blog author, who calls herself "Sunshine," lives in the city of Mosul. In early 2008 it was still a battleground. She described her feelings: "I thought in the beginning of the war that we'll have the life we were told to have, a bright future and live happily ever after, I didn't know there'll be fights and battles in front of my house … I didn't know I'll see dead people in the streets nor hear of all the horrified stories that I hear each day …"

Good police and intelligence work have prevented many attacks in Western countries, as has help from the public. The United States has become a tougher target for Al Qaeda and since 9/11 has not been attacked again on home territory, despite what officials describe as "multiple potential deadly plots" against it. But the US intelligence service predicts that Al Qaeda will try another attack.

The British situation

In Britain, too, terrorist attacks have been successfully foiled. In the summer of 2006, a plot by British-born terrorists to blow up 10 transatlantic aircraft was uncovered before it could be put into operation. In 2007, 41 people were convicted of terrorist offenses in 15 separate cases. But according to Jonathan Evans, the head of Britain's intelligence service, MI5, the terrorist threat is "evolving and has not yet peaked." In a speech made in November 2007, he said that the core Al Qaeda leaders living in tribal areas on the Pakistan-Afghanistan border were encouraging attacks in the UK and people were traveling there for training. Al Qaeda was urging "freelance" groups to operate in East Africa, while Algeria and Somalia were being used as bases for training and planning attacks. In 2006, Evans said MI5 had identified 1,600 individuals in Britain with links to terrorism; by 2007, that number had risen to at least 2,000, with perhaps another 2,000 that MI5 did not know about. Two hundred networks and 30 plots were under investigation.

FOCUS

"Help me get the people out …"

Steve Eldridge is an underground train driver in London. He was standing at the Aldgate station when the bomb went off on July 7, 2005, and he helped to move injured people out of the station. A year later, he recalled the memory of that terrible morning: "There was this loud bang. It was a very short, sharp gust of wind, but it didn't knock us off our feet. Deep down I thought, 'That sounds like a bomb.' I'd never had any experience with a bomb before … One of the passengers came up to me. He had blood all over his face. He said, 'Help me get the people out.'" After the bombing, Eldridge took nine weeks off work to recover. He found it very difficult to go back to driving trains again, but he never thought of changing his job since he says it would have been like running away.

The Muslim experience

Britain is home to 1.6 million Muslims. The overwhelming majority do not agree with the extreme violence that Al Qaeda proposes, but many peace-loving Muslims are unhappy with the foreign policies of Western governments. They also experience discrimination in everyday life. British Asians are twice as likely as white people to be searched by police. Since the July 2005 bombings in London, some people feel that new anti-terrorism laws have turned Britain into a "police state." Although most Muslims oppose terrorism, if they find themselves pushed to the edges of society and isolated, then they are less likely to help in resolving the tensions that exist and more likely to have sympathy with terrorism. Despite some successes in preventing and combating terrorism, much more needs to be done before we can look forward to the future with real optimism.

Students at Millfields Community School in London participate enthusiastically during a class discussion. The interests that we share with other people help to give us a common identity.

FORUM

The extremists are fighting what they believe to be a holy war; others see their actions as unreasonable:

"Your democratically elected governments continually perpetrate atrocities against my people all over the world. Your support makes you directly responsible. We are at war and I am a soldier. Now you too will taste the reality of this situation."

Mohammad Sidique Khan, London suicide bomber, in a pre-recorded video shown on Al Jazeera TV, September 2005

"It's all brainwashing by some wacko scholar who believes his own version of the Qur'an—there is no holy war."

Gous Ali, Muslim boyfriend of bomb victim killed on July 7, 2005

Who do you believe?

Chapter 7

How will terrorism be fought in the future?

The fight against terrorism does not simply involve day-to-day prevention and investigation. The authorities also need to guess what terrorists will do next and keep one step ahead of them. Experts believe that the most significant terrorist threats for the future will involve either the use of weapons of mass destruction or an attack on a country's critical national infrastructure.

Weapons of mass destruction

Much has been written about whether terrorists will "go nuclear" or use biological, chemical, or radiological weapons. The only terrorist attack of this kind to date took place in 1995, when Japanese terrorists released a poisonous gas called sarin in the Tokyo underground system. The attack killed 12 people and seriously injured 50, but it could have been far worse. It is thought that these weapons might be used more often except for technical reasons. It requires highly skilled experts to develop and deploy WMD, and the materials used in their manufacture are hard to obtain and conceal. A 2003 UN report stated that Al Qaeda and some of its associates had tried to obtain chemical and biological weapons and that it was "just a matter of time" before terrorists attempted this type of attack. A few years later, the same fear was echoed by US intelligence.

In November 2007, an important conference on illegal trafficking of nuclear materials was held in Edinburgh, Scotland. Here it was revealed that Al Qaeda had been trying to acquire nuclear material since the 1990s.

In March 1995, rescue workers in Tokyo, Japan, prepare to enter the metro system, where a poison gas attack by a terrorist group called Aum Shinrikyo killed 12 people.

In 2007 in Algiers, North Africa, two car bombs killed over 60 people, including 10 United Nations staff. Responsibility for the attack was claimed by "Al Qaeda in the Land of the Islamic Mahgreb."

A senior British official reported that Al Qaeda was actively seeking high-grade uranium and plutonium in order to detonate a "dirty bomb" in a city such as London or Washington, DC. This bomb would use ordinary explosives to scatter radioactive debris. In August 2007, it was reported that there had been 250 reported thefts or losses of nuclear material around the world in 2006, an increase of about 200 percent since 2002.

Critical infrastructure attacks

Critical infrastructure systems include computerized systems for regulating civil or military aircraft traffic, water and gas supplies, the financial and banking system, electric power grids, and other vital services. A terrorist attack on these could cause untold chaos, because most of us are almost completely dependent on computer systems for the regulation of our lives.

Finally, a serious terrorist threat could result from what is known as the "blowback effect." This refers to the unwanted consequences of a particular action. One consequence of the Iraq invasion may be that Al Qaeda is stronger, not weaker, than it was before. Terrorists who have gained experience fighting in Iraq may return to their home countries—in the Middle East, North Africa or Western Europe—to put into practice what they have learned.

Expert View

US intelligence analysts give a grim warning about terrorist activity in the future:

"We assess that Al Qaeda will continue to try to acquire and employ chemical, biological, radiological, or nuclear material in attacks and would not hesitate to use them if it develops what it deems is sufficient capability."

US National Intelligence Estimate, July 2007

What can we do to stop these new forms of terrorism?

In terms of terrorism prevention, governments need to protect their communications systems with physical and technological defenses. They also need to ensure that they have backup systems to use in the case of cyber-attack. It is very important for governments to cooperate internationally to keep close checks on the manufacture and use of chemical, biological, and radioactive materials.

One of the biggest challenges, especially for Western countries with large Muslim populations such as Britain, is to prevent people's anger from being channeled into terrorist activities. It is therefore important to understand why some young Muslim men have such hatred for the West and what draws them into terrorism. In Britain, the police and intelligence services are trying to recruit more Muslims to help them. In 2007, for the first time ever, the BBC was allowed to interview members of the intelligence services MI5 and MI6. Some of the intelligence officers were Muslim, and when questioned, they said their faith did not conflict with their work.

British Muslims protest during a demonstration in London. The British government must meet the challenge of balancing the rights of its Muslim and non-Muslim citizens.

Governments also need to reduce tensions at the international level, for example, to help Israelis and Palestinians find a peaceful solution to their conflict. As long as there is no homeland for Palestinian people, Muslims around the world will be angry and feel that the situation is unfair. Western governments cannot change their foreign policies because terrorists tell them to, but they can be more sensitive to the feelings of people who are affected by such policies.

Understanding the views of others

Governments can also promote more dialogue and discussion *across* communities. A person's religion is part of who he or she is, but it should not be a barrier to communication. It is important to find interests and identities that unite communities rather than separate them in order to increase people's understanding of one another.

These interests could include hobbies such as soccer, music, flying kites, or playing chess or computer games. If people from different backgrounds and faiths can meet and share common interests, then the differences between them may be seen as valuable and interesting.

Finally, history demonstrates that even terrible conflicts involving terrorism can eventually be resolved. After decades of violence in two very different countries— Northern Ireland and South Africa—peace has at last been achieved through dialogue and compromise. The dialogue in Northern Ireland started secretly and unofficially and took many years. It involved people who had influence with, or enjoyed the respect of, the different sides in the conflict. Representatives of the religious, political, and civil communities looked for common ground on which they could begin to build peace. In 2007, Ian Paisley and Martin McGuinness, two men who used to hate each other, became the first minister

Expert View

A Muslim MI6 officer describes how her loyalty to her faith and her loyalty to her country are inseparable from each other:

"The way I feel is that my duty to God is totally compatible with my duty to my country. I would say extremism in any form is wrong, be that Islamic extremism or any other kind of extremism. I feel very, very strongly that if you are able to do something to make a difference, you should make that difference."

"Yasmin," MI6 officer, speaking on **BBC News,** *November 26, 2007*

and deputy first minister of the new Northern Ireland Assembly in Belfast. Paisley had once described former IRA commander McGuinness as "evil." Once in office, the two men talked to each other all the time and were nicknamed "the Chuckle Brothers" because they were seen laughing together.

First Minister Ian Paisley and Deputy First Minister Martin McGuinness are all smiles after being sworn into office at the Northern Ireland Assembly.

Meeting and talking

In 1989, the new president of South Africa, F. W. de Klerk, realized that international public opinion was completely opposed to apartheid and that the regime could not last. So he invited his "enemy," Nelson Mandela, to have talks with him. He showed Mandela respect, and the two men began to talk as equals. In 1990, after 27 years in prison, Mandela was released and began to work for peace. With the support and involvement of religious leaders such as Desmond Tutu, archbishop of Cape Town, the South African government set up the Truth and Reconciliation Commission. This allowed people of all races to describe their experiences of the terrible things they had done or that had been had done to them during the apartheid years. Desmond Tutu described black South Africans as "wounded healers" because of all they had suffered.

Choosing peace

Events in South Africa and Northern Ireland prove that hatred and conflict can be overcome and that former enemies can live in peace. But these things can only be achieved through dialogue. There are no magic recipes for peace, of course, and one cannot imagine the president of the United States sitting down to talk

In March 2005, on the first anniversary of the Madrid train bombings, members of Madrid's Islamic community observe a minute of silence in front of a banner in Spanish and Arabic that reads "Everyone Against Terrorism."

with Osama bin Laden. But it is the duty of individual leaders or representatives of communities in conflict to explore the space for common ground. They may need the help of a mediator, an outsider with no personal involvement in the conflict, who can talk to both sides and bring them together. Mediators have been used in many peace talks, including in Northern Ireland.

Defeating terrorism depends on communication and on respecting individual and cultural differences. It means finding ways to reduce inequalities between people, better ways of living together in a crowded world, and better ways of sharing its resources. Terrorism will probably never disappear entirely. There will always be people who feel anger and a sense of injustice and who will decide, somewhere in the world, that violence is the way to change things. There can be military victories against terrorism, but there can never be military solutions to it. Terrorism will only cease when those in whose name it is being fought decide to reject it; when the hearts and minds of a population turn away from violence and start seeking dialogue.

Memorial lights shine at Ground Zero, the site of the collapsed twin towers of the World Trade Center in New York. A new skyscraper called Freedom Tower is now under construction. Three other towers will be built to form a semicircle around a memorial to the victims of 9/11.

FORUM

Experts have very different ideas about the way in which the war on terrorism can be won:

"Overall, I think that the most suitable methods of beating this global terrorist movement are through extremely good intelligence, effective and clear law enforcement structures with strong international cooperation, but also, unfortunately, some military measures in places where law enforcement structures are ineffective."

Gavin Proudley, UK terrorism expert, July 2007

"Our most effective defense against terrorism will not come from surveillance, concrete barriers, metal detectors, or new laws. It will come from our own virtue, our courage, our continued dedication to the ideals of a free society."

Brian M. Jenkins, US terrorism expert, October 2007

Do you agree with either of these views?

Glossary

apartheid Literally "apartness"; describes the regime in South Africa from 1948 to 1991 that officially discriminated against non-white citizens.

atrocities Cruel and terrible actions.

cell A small unit or group.

civilian A person who is not a member of the military or the police.

coalition An alliance or partnership between countries or political parties, usually for a specific period.

Cold War A period of tension and hostility between the United States and its allies and the Soviet Union and its allies that lasted from 1945 until 1989.

communism A political and economic system in which all factories, farms, and resources are owned by the state.

democracy A system of government where every adult citizen has the right to vote for a political party of his or her choice.

democratic Belonging to a democracy, where everyone has a say in decision making.

encrypt To convert information into a secret language or code.

European Commission A group of people representing each EU country, who are responsible for ensuring that the policies agreed to between them are put into practice.

European Union (EU) An economic and political association of 27 European countries.

federal Concerning the central government of a country.

firewall A computer protection system.

genocide The deliberate killing of a very large number of people from a particular ethnic group or nation.

guerrilla A member of a small, independent group fighting against a larger, regular army.

indiscriminate Making no distinctions, haphazard.

infidel An unbeliever or a person whose religion is different from those describing him or her as an infidel.

infiltrate To gain access to a group secretly.

insurgency A violent uprising.

intelligence service An organization that collects information that can be used to defend a country from harm and attack.

kamikaze A Japanese word meaning "divine wind" used to describe the Japanese aircraft that made deliberate suicide attacks on enemy targets during World War II.

left wing Describes a political position held by those who generally favor the working class or less well-off people in society.

martyr Someone who chooses to die for a cause or set of beliefs.

militants People involved in (usually armed) conflict.

militia An armed group.

monarchy A nation ruled by a king or queen. A monarchy is usually hereditary, meaning the right to rule passes to the eldest child or nearest heir of the monarch.

reconciliation A bringing together in peace, an overcoming of hostility.

republic A nation ruled by a chosen or elected representative rather than a monarch.

republican Belonging to a republic.

right wing Describes a political position held by those who generally favor traditional values, free enterprise, and private ownership.

sharia law Strict Islamic law based on the teachings of the Qur'an.

Soviet Union Also known as the Union of Soviet Socialist Republics (USSR), the Soviet Union was established in 1922 following the Russian Revolution. It was a republic made up of countries in eastern Europe and central and northern Asia, with Moscow as its capital city. Following the end of the Cold War in 1990, the Soviet Union was dismantled.

suffrage The right to vote.

surveillance A technique of investigation that involves watching a person and monitoring his or her movements.

Taliban Originally a group of religious scholars, later the ruling group in Afghanistan from 1996 to 2001.

United Nations (UN) An international organization set up following World War II to promote peace, security, cooperation, and understanding.

wiretap A device that allows telephone conversations to be overheard and recorded.

Further information

Books
Specialized reading:
Gearty, Conor. *Terror.* Orion, 1997.

Hoffman, Bruce. *Inside Terrorism*. Columbia University Press, 2006.

Richardson, Louise. *What Terrorists Want: Understanding the Enemy, Containing the Threat.* Random House, 2006.

General reading:
Commonwealth Secretariat. *Civil Paths to Peace: Report of the Commonwealth Commission on Respect and Understanding*. Commonwealth Secretariat, 2007.

Mandela, Nelson. *Long Walk to Freedom: The Autobiography of Nelson Mandela.* Holt Rinehart & Winston, 2000.

Rosen, Andrew. *Rise Up Women! Militant Campaign of the Women's Social and Political Union, 1903-14.* Routledge Kegan & Paul, 1974.

Websites
www.whitehouse.gov/infocus/homeland/index.html

The interactive website of the White House/Department of Homeland Security provides information on the current status of the US war on terrorism worldwide, gives the current threat level of terrorism in the United States, and lists contacts at the White House to e-mail with questions about terrorism.

www.dni.gov/press_releases/20070717_release.pdf

The report from the US National Intelligence Council on the terrorist threat to the United States.

www.unodc.org/unodc/en/terrorism/index.html

Describes the work of the United Nations Office on Drugs and Crime in preventing terrorism; includes information about 13 global conventions against terrorism.

http://europa.eu/scadplus/leg/en/s22011.htm

Details of how European Union countries are cooperating to combat terrorism.

www.crisisgroup.org

Website of the International Crisis Group, an independent, non-profit, non-governmental organization working to prevent and resolve deadly conflict worldwide.

Index

Entries in **bold** are for pictures.